AF086470

Vv

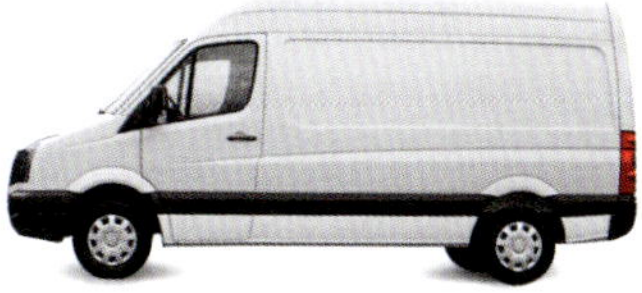

Ransom

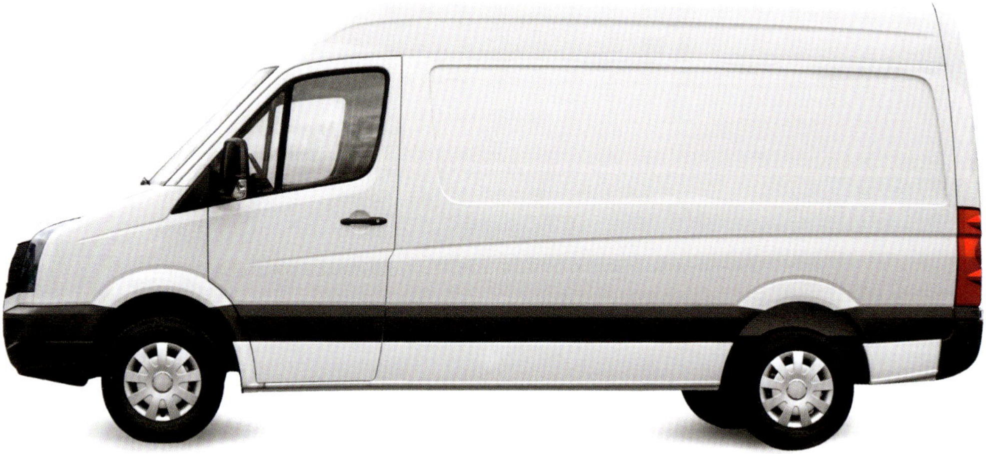

van

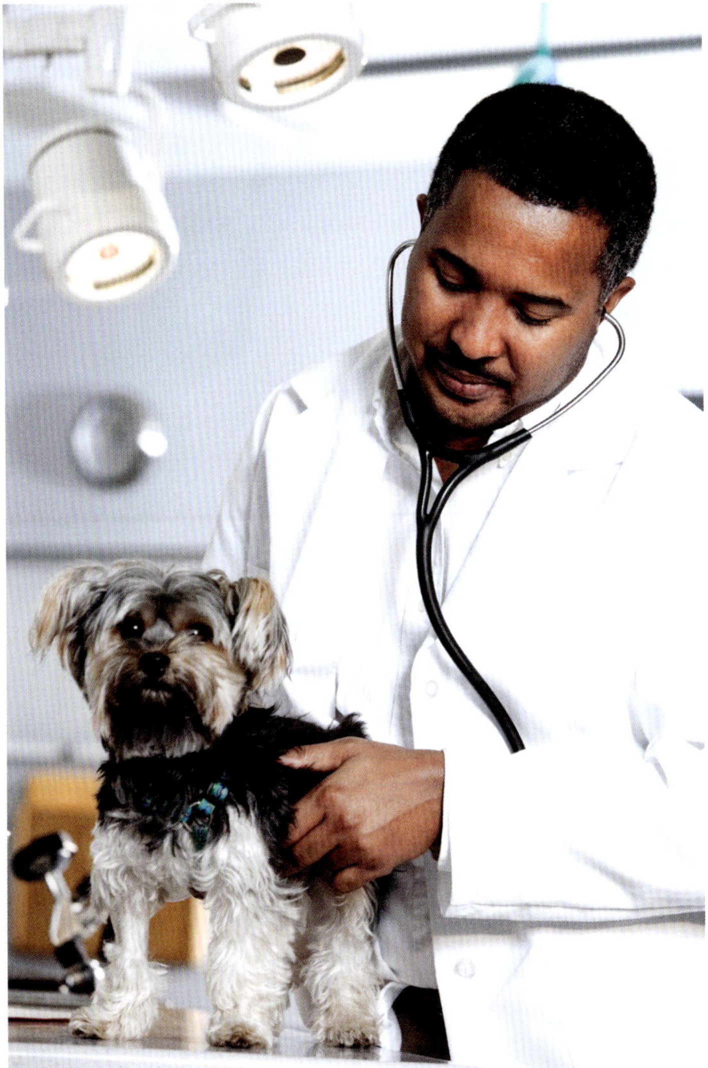

vet

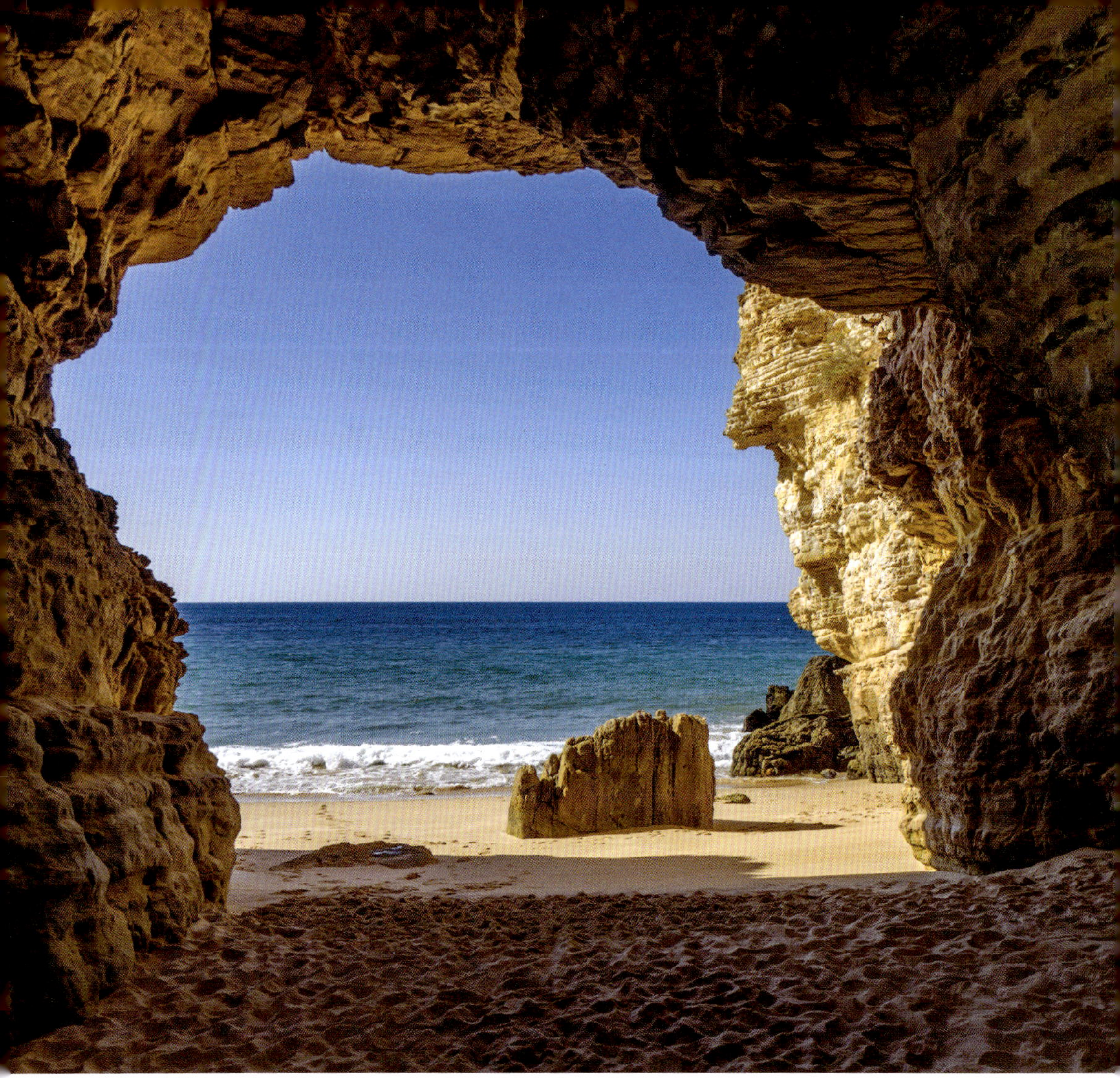

cave

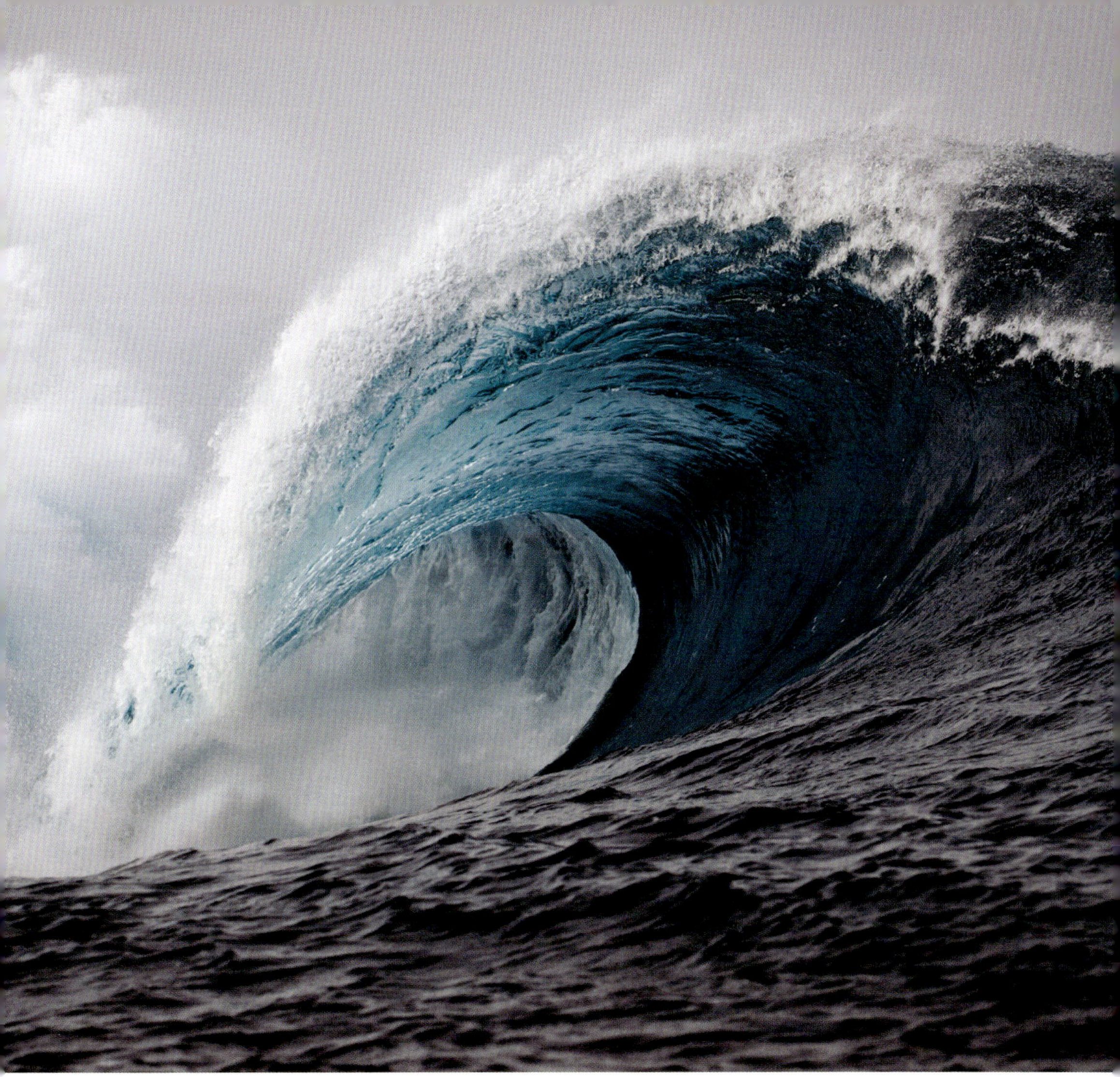

wave

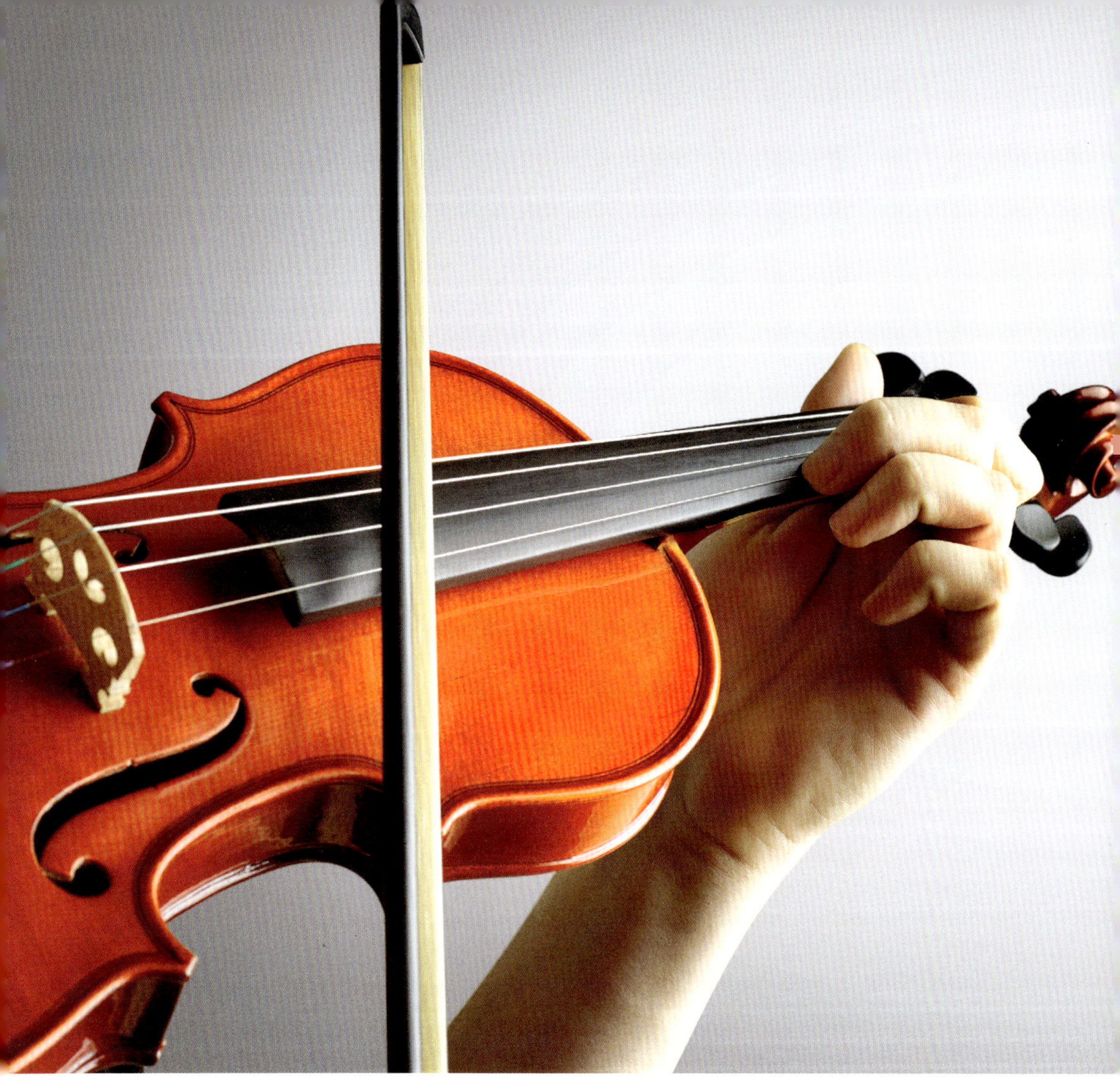

violin

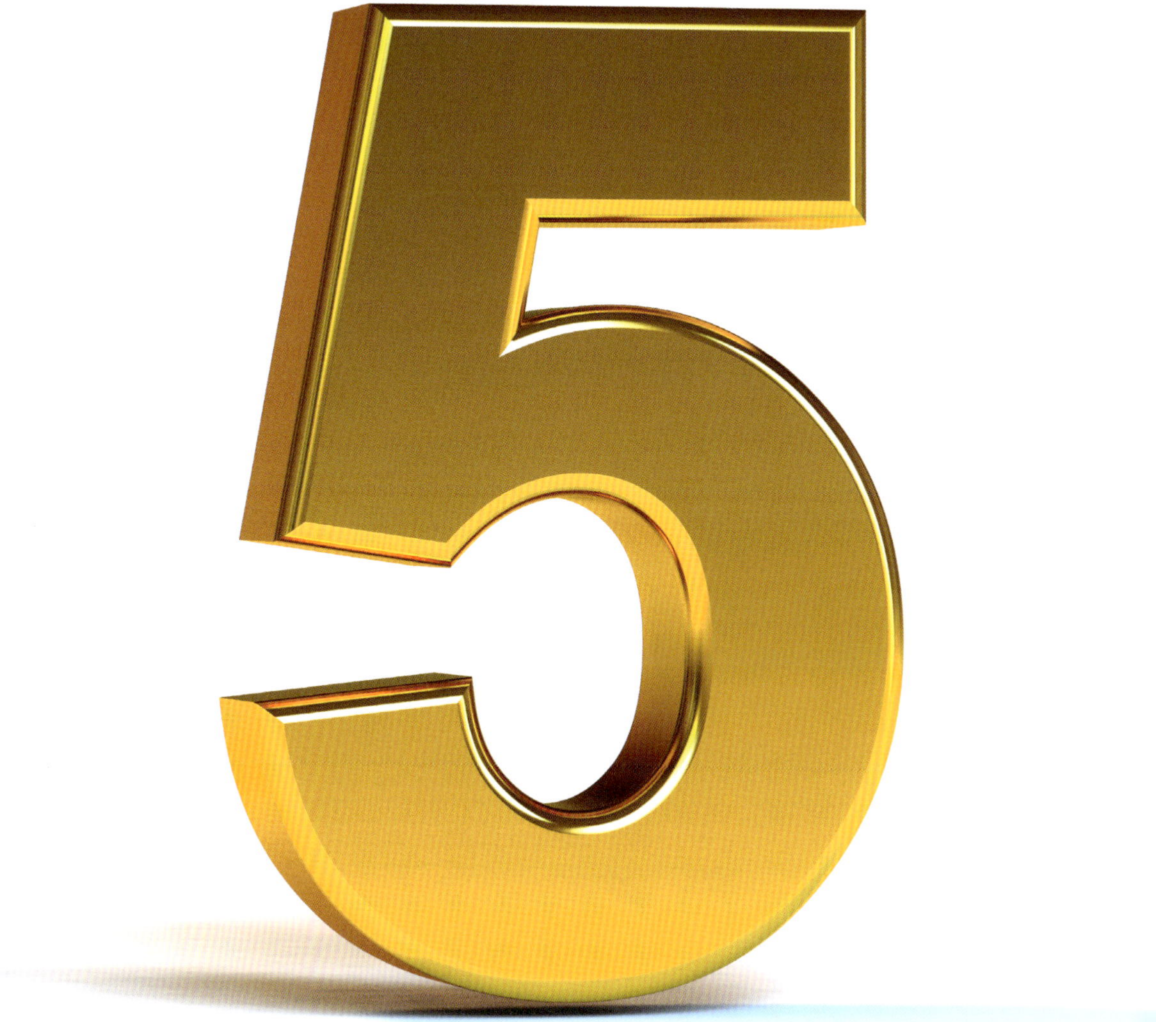

five

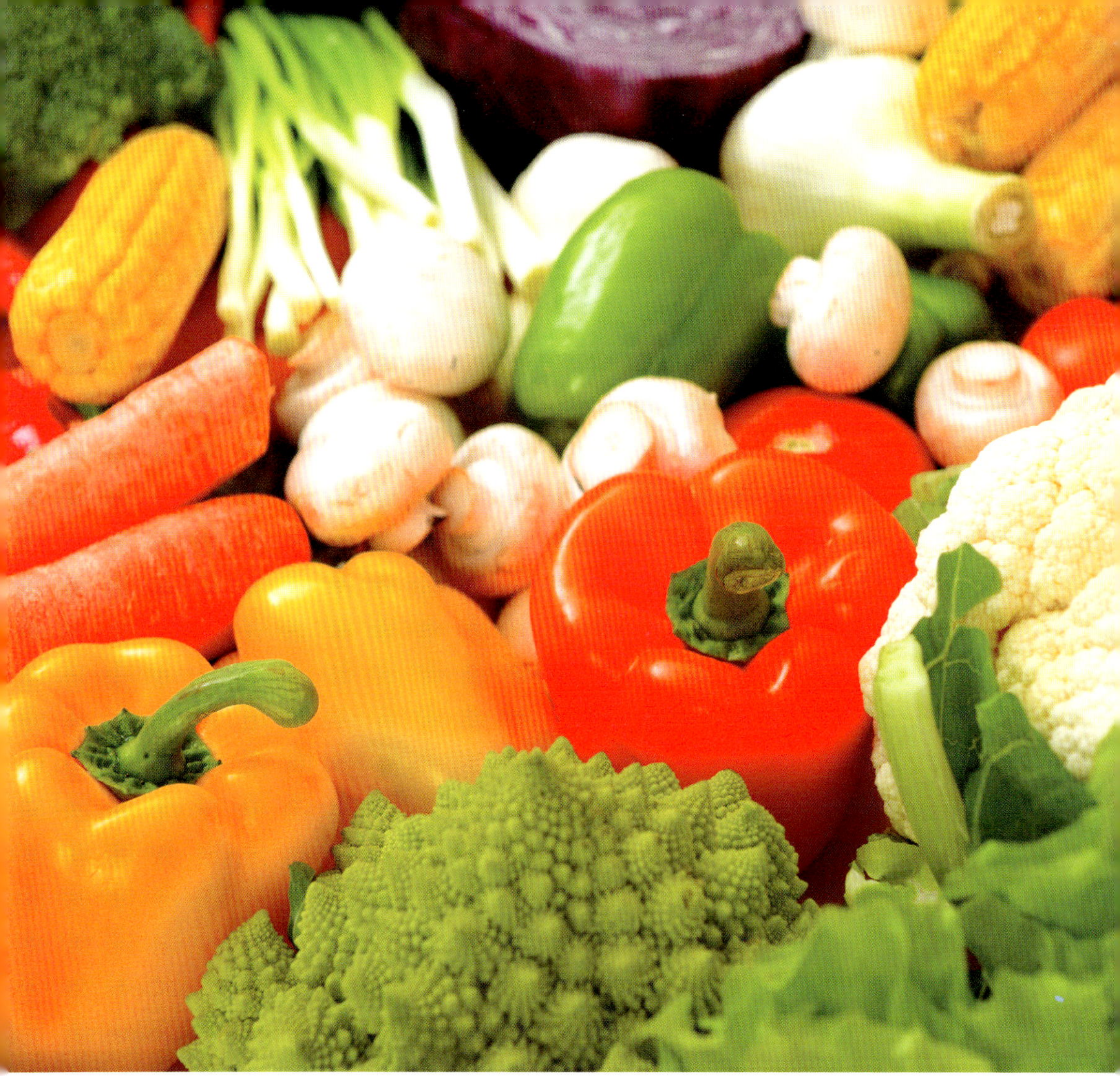

vegetables

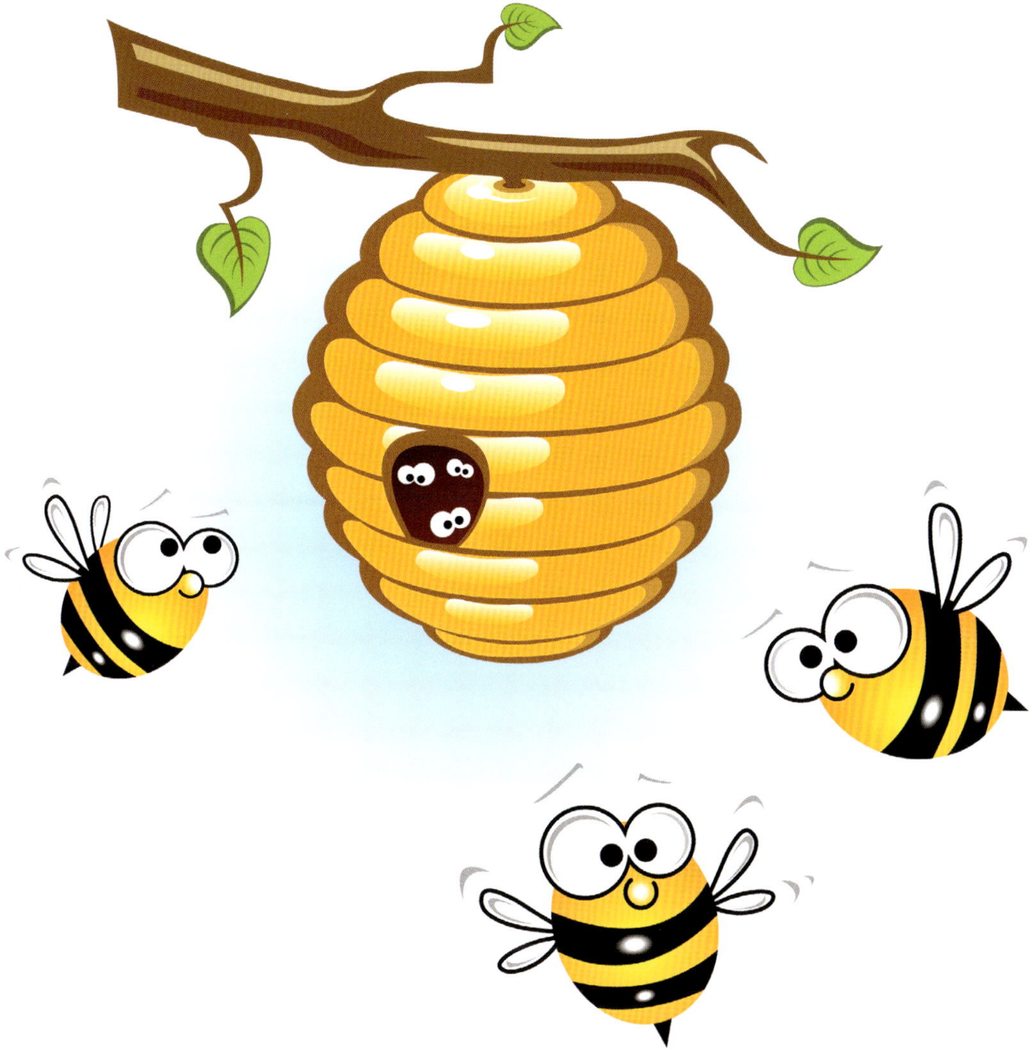

beehive

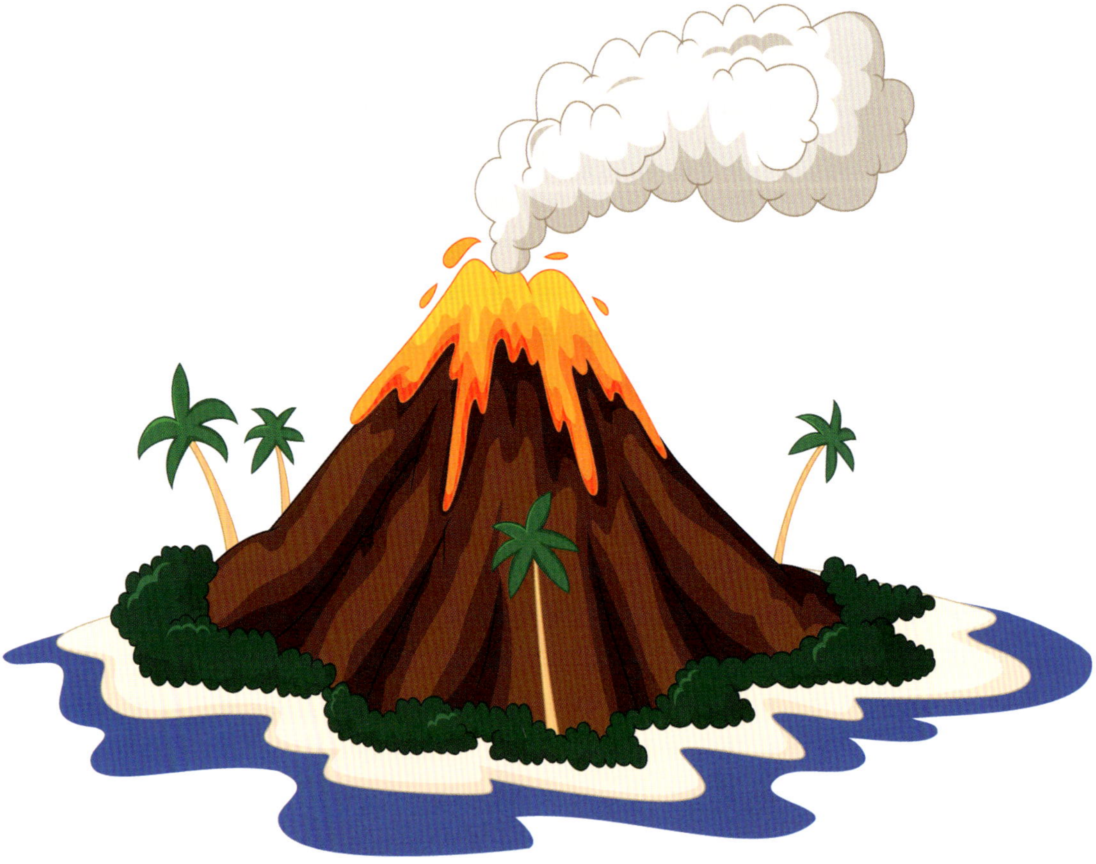

v v v v

v v v v

Vv

van

vet

cave

wave

violin

five

vegetables

beehive